THE
COLORADO RIVER

Featuring the Photography of Chris Swan
CLB 1502
© 1986 Illustrations and text: Colour Library Books Ltd.,
    Guildford, Surrey, England.
Text filmsetting by Acesetters Ltd., Richmond, Surrey, England.
Printed in Spain.
All rights reserved.
1986 edition published by Crescent Books, distributed by Crown Publishers, Inc.
ISBN 0 517 601915
h g f e d c b a
Dep.Leg. B-5.254-86

THE
COLORADO RIVER

Text by
BARBARA COOLEY

CRESCENT BOOKS
NEW YORK

In the Beginning...

"Long ago, there was a great wise chief, who mourned the death of his wife, and would not be comforted until Ta-vweats, one of the Indian gods, came to him, and told him she was in a happier land, and offered to take hime there, that he might see for himself, if, upon his return, he would cease to mourn. The great chief promised. Then Ta-vweats made a trail through the mountains that intervene between that beautiful land, the balmy region in the great west, and this, the desert home of the poor Nú-ma.

"This trail was the canyon gorge of the Colorado. Through it he led him; and, when they had returned the deity exacted from the chief a promise that he would tell no one of the joys of that land, lest, through discontent with the circumstances of this world, they should desire to go to heaven. Then he rolled a river into the gorge, a mad, raging stream, that should engulf any that might attempt to enter thereby.

"More than once have I been warned by the Indians not to enter this canyon. They considered it disobedience to the gods and contempt for their authority, and believed that it would surely bring upon me their wrath."

These words were written by Major John Wesley Powell, the one-armed veteran of the Civil War, who led nine men in four boats on an epic journey over rapids considered impassable, to chart unexplored sections of the Colorado River and its surrounding canyons.

On August 30, 1869, 13 weeks after the expedition left Green River Station in Wyoming Territory, the Major, with only one boat and five crew members, emerged below Grand Wash Cliffs (the western tip of the Grand Canyon) to find men fishing with nets for their remains.

Before the trip was over, Powell and his party would lose most of their food, their extra clothing and blankets, and four men. Frank Goodman quit the expedition after all his clothes went down with one boat at Disaster Falls and, three-quarters of the way through the Grand Canyon, the Howland brothers and William Dunn announced that it was madness to attempt the rapids up ahead, and that they would climb out of the canyon instead.

Powell tried to persuade Captain Howland to stay. The entry in the Major's journal, dated August 27, reads: "All night long, I pace up and down a little path... by the river. Is it wise to go on? I go to the boats again, to look at our rations. I feel satisfied that we can get over the danger immediately before us; what they may be below I know not... I am not sure that we can climb out of the canyon here, and, when at the top of the wall, I know enough of the country to be certain that it is a desert of rock and sand, between this and the nearest Mormon town... But for years I have been contemplating the trip. To leave the exploration unfinished, to say that there is a part of the canyon which I cannot explore, having already almost accomplished it, is more than I am willing to acknowledge, and I determine to go on."

The next morning there was a silent breakfast and a tearful goodbye. The three departing men helped the others to lift two of the boats around the first part of the rapid. (The last boat was left behind for lack of a crew.) Then, laden with rifles and shotguns, a letter from Major Powell to his wife, a duplicate record of the voyage and J.C. Sumner's watch, with instructions to send it on to his sister should he not survive, the Howland men and Mr. Dunn climbed a crag and were off.

Three days later, Powell and the remaining crew achieved the honor of being the first to navigate the Colorado's canyons and to live to tell the tale. The three men who climbed out were killed by Shivwit Indians not long after they left the canyon.

Of course, Powell wasn't the first man to penetrate the mysteries of the Grand Canyon. By 12000 B.C. Paleo-Indians hunted in the Colorado River Basin for mammoth, bison and sloth. The Desert Culture people who followed them left behind paintings in Utah's Horseshoe Canyon and animal figurines in caves along Grand Canyon's Redwall Limestone cliffs.

One of their descendents, the Anasazi, arrived around 600 A.D. In addition to hunting they survived on a spring harvest of squash and beans, and a later harvest within the canyons along the banks of the Colorado. It is believed that a drought which lasted many years drove the Anasazi out of the canyon in 1200.

During the 1869 expedition, Powell reported finding Indian etchings on the face of a cliff, great quantities of arrow heads and flint chips, and several stone houses. He noted that between the rooms of one L-shaped house there was a deep excavation, an underground chamber or "kiva," where Indians performed religious ceremonies.

Thanks to Powell and later explorers, several hundred Anasazi sites have been recorded in Grand Canyon National Park. An area of particular interest for today's hiker and river runner lies along the 20-mile stretch of the Colorado between Nankoweap Creek, in the lower end of Marble Gorge, and Unkar Creek. South of the mouth of Nankoweap Creek – 500 feet up, in the west canyon wall – the Anasazi carved out and reinforced with masonry a series of grain storage bins.

For the Anasazi and other contemporary Indian tribes, as well as for those who followed, life consisted of adapting to an extremely rugged environment. The deities and ceremonies in their religion fostered a coexistence, a harmony with nature. But they couldn't explain the white man – and his terrible hunger for gold.

Why, the Hopi and Zuni must have wondered, was the warrior chief known as Francisco Vásquez de Coronado leading great armies across the vast plains? Perhaps the Indians hoped to send the man packing when they talked about a mighty river to the west. After Coronado showed great interest – nothing matched a river for moving troops

and supplies – the Hopi led Captain Cárdenas and his small party on a 20-day march through the desert. The Spaniards stepped out onto the south rim of the Grand Canyon and became the first white men to see the Colorado River hemmed in – like a thin piece of thread – between foreboding cliffs. Even then, size and space proved illusory: after climbing a third of the way down to the river, three soldiers exclaimed – upon reaching the rim again – that the rocks they encountered were much taller than they appeared from the top, taller yet than the Tower of Seville!

In the end, Coronado's campaign failed. Like Cortés, he found no emeralds, no El Dorado, no legendary cities of gold. But, during the next 250 years, many Spanish missionaries would criss-cross the Southwest in a zealous quest to convert the Zuñi and Hopi to "the one true God." Following ancient Indian trails or beating down new ones, these friars could also claim to have seen Grand Canyon. But they were only interested in geography in so far as it helped or hindered the salvation of man's soul.

The Colorado and Grand Canyon remained a mystery – a blank space on North American maps – until men like prospector James White told horrible tales about escaping from Indians, and tossing helplessly on hastily-made rafts for countless days through dark, steep canyons and whirling rapids. That was in 1867. The River and its canyons had long been the stuff of Indian legend; now it was grabbing hold of the white man's imagination. Maybe because there were lots of tales, but few facts. Nevertheless, when Major Powell recounted his trip in a series of articles for *Scribner's Monthly* magazine, he created a sensation. From then on, and forever after, the Colorado River and its Grand Canyon entered the realm of American folklore.

Early residents added local color. The Kolb brothers lived on the south rim of the Grand Canyon and ran a photography business, taking pictures of tourists who were riding mules down Bright Angel Trail. Photographer, artist, explorer, lecturer and canyon enthusiast, Emery Kolb ran his last rapid in December 1976, at the age of 96.

One couple, Glen and Bessie Hyde, chose to spend their honeymoon boating through the Grand Canyon. On October 28, 1928, they left Utah on the Green River. They navigated down the Green, entered the Colorado, and proceeded into the Marble Gorge. They visited Emery Kolb on November 15. He urged them to take along life preservers. They declined, and returned to the river. Rangers found their boat, right side up, with 14 inches of water in the bottom. Bessie's diary, camera and other items were in the boat. The couple were never found.

In 1949, Bert Loper also chose to die on the river. A long-time river guide, Bert was one month shy of 80 years old and suffering from heart trouble when he embarked on his last run. His boat capsized in one of the rapids. Fellow travelers recovered Bert's boat, but his body had somehow slipped out of the life preserver and disappeared. Bert had always said that he wanted to die on the river and be buried on its banks. He got at least part of his wish.

Some people will tell you that seeing the Grand Canyon is like stepping off the edge of the earth. Others will say: "How can you describe it – it's so incomprehensible?" Words are like the tip of the iceberg shafting the sea; they can only hint at the powerful emotions swelling below the surface. An early guide book on the Grand Canyon gave up on trying to describe what tourists see there. The only way to do it, said the guide, is to quote what the average tourist says on first seeing the place: "My God!"

If the Colorado River was only known as the sculptor of the Grand Canyon that would be enough to make it a mighty river. Yet the Colorado is more – much more.

Some have compared her to the Nile in Egypt, because both carry the promise of life to desert country. Here the comparison ends: less than half as long as the Nile and draining half the million square miles watered by the Nile, the Colorado has fused itself into the heart and soul and blood of the American Southwest.

The Colorado is the river bank Indian who, waiting for the annual spring flood waters to recede, planted in the mud flats and watched his crops mature before the soil dried out.

The Colorado is the Anasazi woman who cultivated her fields near natural springs... who built low stone walls to direct the storm waters rushing down granite funnels... and paved and lined with adobe a 300-mile system of ditches, diversion dams and reservoirs to store water.

The Colorado is the Mormon in Utah who began building canals in the 1850s, and also the thousands of farmers who, following Horace Greeley's advice to *Go West, young man,* rushed into California's newly created Imperial Valley.

For close to 150 years the Colorado River has permeated and directed the political, economic and emotional history of the people who live in its basin. Now the land *is* the river. And the river is the land.

The River and the Land
Ten thousand feet above sea level, in the snow-covered Rocky Mountains, in a craggy landscape thick with lakes, waterfalls and forests of spruce, aspen and fir, the Colorado begins its 1,450-mile journey to the Gulf of California.

Joined by seven northern tributaries, and descending at a rate of 7.9 feet per mile (a descent 25 times greater than that of the Mississippi), the river winds southward in a series of great bends across the high plateaus of Colorado, southeastern Utah and northwestern Arizona.

"You must not think," Major Powell wrote, "of a mountain range as a line of peaks standing on a plain, but as a broad platform many miles wide, from which mountains have been carved by the waters. You must conceive, too, that this plateau is cut by gulches and canyons in many directions, and that beautiful valleys are scattered about at different altitudes." The plateaus which Powell describes encompass 130,000 of the 240,000 square miles drained by the Colorado

River system. Scientists say that these plains were originally under water possibly as many as seven times before inland oceans permanently withdrew, leaving behind layers of horizontal sedimentary rock.

On the plateaus, the tundra of the north country yields first to the cinammon-bark ponderosa pine, whose extensive root system allows it to tolerate drier areas, then to scruffy, twisted junipers and pinyon pines (masters at survival in a semi-arid desert), and finally to sagebrush, cactus and the occasional willow and cottonwood tree growing alongside a stream.

At the southern edge of Utah, the plateau drops abruptly onto an oblong terrace known as the Arizona Strip. It's a desolate region so cut off from the rest of Arizona that its residents historically felt more kinship with Utah than to their native state. In the Strip there are few paved roads, just lots of trails leading nowhere, or to sun-baked ledges where a few paces forward will plunge you into a 2,802-foot hole in the earth. The Grand Canyon's Toroweap Point is one of these places: a ledge on the north rim topping a narrow gorge of orange and russet colored walls, too steep to climb and molded long, long ago by the lava that erupted from volcanic action in this western portion of the canyon. About this place Major Powell wrote: "What a conflict of water and fire there must have been here! Just imagine a river of molten rock running down into a river of melted snow. What a seething and boiling of waters; what clouds of steam rolled into the Heavens."

But the plateau country is more than shrill sunlight, gaunt rock and the thin bead of the Colorado far below. East of the Arizona Strip, the Kaibab Forests stretch along the north rim and, across the canyon, along the south rim as well. A distance of 10 miles from rim to rim seems to keep the Kaibab squirrel in the northern forest and nowhere else in the world. And here, at 8,000 feet above sea level – in the colder weather and heavier snowfalls – the Aspen tree thrives.

On the lower south rim, trees more effective at water conservation dominate: along the edge, pinyon pine and Utah juniper; further back, where there's more soil and moisture, ponderosa pine, Gambel oak, Yucca, mountain mahogany and cliffrose.

Ravens and turkey vultures coast in the thermal updrafts. Swifts and swallows, white-tailed and mule deer, coyote, gray fox, bobcat and the occasional mountain lion all populate the rim forests.

It's a population that wasn't always balanced in quite the same way. At the turn of the century, James T. "Uncle Jim" Owens, warden of what was then called the Grand Canyon Game Reserve, exterminated 500 mountain lions. Uncle Jim "executed" them with the best of intentions; but with the natural predator of the deer removed, herds swelled to 100,000. A deer drive was organized: several thousand animals would be driven down the Nankoweap Trail, across the Colorado River and up the Tanner Trail to the south rim. Over 100 men participated in the roundup. Since then, natural attrition has thinned the herd to about 10,000, a number which appears to be compatible with the environment.

Below the south rim the plateaus continue. This is the home of Indian Nations like the Navajo and Hualapai, of the Painted Desert, and of sagebrush and desert scrub. This is land touched by the river as it courses south, forming part of the boundary between Nevada and Arizona, and then between Arizona and California. Here, in southern Arizona, the Gila River offers the Colorado what little water it has left after crossing a land moistened by three inches of rain a year and scorched by hot winds and a summer temperature which can reach 120 degrees Fahrenheit.

Below Yuma, the river flows on through the tip of northern Mexico and empties in the Gulf of California.

The Early River
The Red River, the Grand Colorado, the Grand: over the centuries, the river was known by many names. It was

Colorado's United States Congressman Edward Taylor who succeeded, in 1921, in defining, for all future atlases and, more important, for the pending discussions concerning how much river water each state should have, that "his" state, and not Wyoming, contained the headwaters of the Colorado, his state, which had obviously been named for the river.

Almost 400 years earlier, the Spaniards couldn't decide what to call the Colorado either. Francisco de Ulloa – sailing north from Acapulco under orders from Cortés – discovered the mouth of the river in 1539. Since it was St. Andrew's Day, Ulloa named the river for the saint. A year later, Hernando de Alarcón, captain of Coronado's supply ships, called the Colorado *The River of Good Guidance*. It was finally the colonist and explorer Juan de Oñate who, in 1598, named the river for its muddy, red color. Actually, Oñate was referring to a tributary, the Little Colorado, but somehow the parent river acquired the same name.

For a long time, the Colorado was a muddy, red river. Prior to the construction of Glen Canyon Dam in northern Arizona, the Colorado carried an average of 500,000 tons of sand and sediment downriver every day. After 1964, the daily silt load lightened to 80,000 tons. Now, depending on the mud content, and whether it's been raining in the east or southeast, the Colorado appears blue, green or brown.

It is this load of silt, carried from 10,000 feet to sea level at an average speed of seven miles per hour, which explains the river's part in the creation of the multi-colored, multi-layered canyons through which it flows.

The Colorado has created a unique landscape, one that was too rugged for cities or ports ever to take hold. Only the lower part, below Hoover Dam, is easily navigated. Today, in 15 miles known as the Parker Strip, marinas, resorts and restaurants dot the shoreline, and speedboats zigzag between California and Arizona. But even this part of the river has never been used to transport people and goods; not the way the Mississippi or the Hudson historically has.

Even at its southern borders the Colorado was always too unpredictable: overflowing in turbulent spring floods, or drying out, in time of drought, to a shallow stream filled with sandbars and snags.

In August 1540, Captain Alarcón soon found that out. Facing the tidal bore which had forced Ulloa to turn back the year before, Alarcón ordered his ships into a wall of foam and waves which grew higher and higher as the gulf's incoming tide fought the river's outflow. Sheets of water washed over and battered the decks of his grounded vessels until the incoming tide lifted the ships and carried them into the river's estuary.

The current was fierce. The captain transferred his crew to two launches, which the men tried to row and pull upstream, but the mud in the river and the soft banks caving in underfoot made the task impossible.

Not so for the Cocopa Indians, who had been watching the struggle hidden behind the delta brush. A deal was struck: hundreds of naked, brightly painted Indians pulled the flotilla forward in hot desert sun for 15 days. They stopped when they learned of an attack by the white man at the village of Háwikuh. By this time, Alarcón – ordered by Coronado to transport supplies upriver for a rendezvous with the land column – had also learned of the battle. He asked his men to volunteer, but no one was willing to cross the desert with a message for Coronado. In September, Alarcón turned around a few miles below the junction of the Colorado and Gila rivers. Retreating back toward the gulf, he just missed Coronado's messenger.

The New Invader
The Spaniards came and saw and tried to conquer. But, like many an occupying army, they didn't change the lay of the land. Forgotten by the white man, the Colorado flowed on, abandoned to its own will until 1821, when Mexico won independence from Spain and opened the doors of its northern frontiers. Then a new breed of men invaded the

rivers of the Colorado system: men who came from east of the Missouri; men who were trappers, traders, hunters, guides and Indian scouts; men who were searching for beaver.

Beaver was a kind of currency: 80 skins to a pack weighing 100 pounds was worth $500. Since the late 1790s, every well-dressed male boasted of owning a beaver hat, wide-brimmed or stove-pipe, and it wasn't long before American and European beaver stocks were depleted.

So the trapper moved westward. In dug-out canoes and bull-boats he discovered the land: the valleys and the streams, the mesas, the mountains and the canyons in the land of the Colorado.

Like the canoe, the bull-boat was made on the spot. William Ashley, lieutenant-governor of the new state of Missouri, and his crew of trappers fashioned the frame of their flat-bottomed bull-boats out of cottonwood and willow trees. The frame was covered with buffalo skins sewn together and waterproofed by a mix of buffalo tallow and ashes. In 1825 the Ashley party ran the rapids, portaging their boats when the river became impassable. At one point, Ashley later reported, they went without food for six days and, menaced with the dread that they'd never find their way out of the canyon, swore that they would have soon eaten one of their own.

A year later, a former miner named James Ohio Pattie told of a similar adventure. After joining a party of French-American trappers heading for the "Red River," Pattie said they "reached a point of the river where the mountains shut in so close... that we were compelled to climb a mountain... the river still in sight, and at an immense depth beneath us..." The party moved along the chasm's rim for 13 days, arriving "where the river emerges from these horrid mountains, which so cage it up, as to deprive all human beings of the ability to... make use of its waters."

Was Pattie the first white man to navigate the upper Colorado? Historians couldn't be sure. Only one thing was certain, for the Spaniard and now, for the American, too: the Colorado, swift and strong and a natural corridor from north to south, seemed forever unattainable.

The fur trade disintegrated in the late 1830s. But by then the trapper had opened the quarter-million-square-mile basin of the Colorado River. In turn, the overland routes by which caravans brought him supplies, the trading posts, the blacksmith shops and canteens, his Indian woman and mixed-blood children, all these bound the trapper to the land. And he stayed on. Like Kit Carson, he led government troops to the last strongholds of the Indian. He guided prospectors and wagon trains. He killed buffalo to feed the passing emigrants.

For this was a land on the move. Every emigrant was fired by a dream of his own. Mormons were among the first. From 1846-1856, 76,0000 American and European converts to the new Church of Jesus Christ of Latter Day Saints emigrated to the Mormon empire in the territory of Utah. The Mormons dreamed about becoming a separate nation. Their dream dissolved when Utah achieved statehood.

The prospector was fired by a dream, too. In 1849, untold numbers crossed into California, each one certain that he would find the mother lode. A decade later over 100,000 "fifty-niners" lumbered toward Colorado, the canvas on their covered wagon blazing: "Pike's Peak or Bust." A year later, their tattered wagon sheets sighed, "Busted, by Gosh." Still they came. Towns grew up and towns died, and the miners moved on to Arizona, New Mexico and Nevada.

Seth Tanner, an early Mormon pioneer, helped organize the Little Colorado Mining District. Today, the nine-mile trail, leading from Lipan Point on the Grand Canyon's south rim to the river below, bears his name, even though it was long used by Hopi and Havasupai Indians to reach salt deposits near the Little Colorado River.

Sometimes the route is called the Tanner-French Trail, because prospector Franklin French used it, too. French enjoyed telling listeners how difficult it was to get his donkeys to haul lumber down the 7,300-foot trail to his mine by the river. To illustrate, he'd recall the time he resorted to extraordinary measures: knowing that whiskey could make men do what they wouldn't attempt when sober, he liberally added some to the mules' water supply. The animals made it down with the planks. But, added French, you never saw a more remorseful lot of mules the following morning.

Lewis Boucher, nicknamed "The Hermit," worked copper and asbestos mines until innovations in processing low grade copper made hauling the 70 percent pure ore out of the canyon unprofitable.

George Riley, a member of Major Powell's second canyon expedition, discovered gold in the Grand Canyon. A minor rush lasted four months; there wasn't enough to justify the hard work.

Nevertheless, gold was important in the exploration of the Colorado River. After the United States-Mexican War of 1846, America gained a large part of Mexico's northern territory: Grand Canyon country and almost the full length of the Colorado. And, since where individuals go government soon follows, it wasn't long before a fort was built in Yuma, Arizona, to protect prospectors from Indian attack as they ferried across the Colorado into California.

The fort had to be supplied, and in 1851, George Alonzo Johnson stocked his schooner and started upriver. Soon stalled by the river's swift current, he resorted to flatboats and poled the supplies to Yuma.

The next year, James Turnball inaugurated the first steamboat on the Colorado: the 65-foot-long *Uncle Sam*. It had a sidewheel and it steamed 120 miles from the mouth of the river to Yuma, bringing supplies to the fort in 15 days.

Other steamers were soon transporting goods and people along the lower Colorado. But after the turn of the century the railroad would prove that it could carry passengers and freight much cheaper than the cost of a voyage up and through the gulf.

Popular water travel stopped; exploration did not. In the 1850s, the Federal Territorial Government of Utah faced hostile Mormons. If the army was to be sent to re-enforce authority, additional supply routes had to be found.

Army Lieutenant Joseph Ives was ordered to determine how far steamboats could navigate up the Colorado and to explore the river and its tributaries in the area of the Grand Canyon. On December 31, 1857, Lieut. Ives began his expedition at the river's mouth on the steamboat *Explorer*. (That same day, George Johnson steamed out of Yuma in a desperate race to be the first to find the head of steamer navigation.)

Again and again the men from *Explorer* came to shore in skiffs, wrapped themselves in rope and proceeded to tow the steamboat off another sandbar. Progress was slow. The expedition's physician and geologist, Dr. John Strong Newberry, wrote: "Day after day as we slowly crawl along up the muddy Colorado confined to a little tucked up over-loaded, over-crowded steamer with no retreat from the cold, heat, wind or drifting sand, and nothing but the monotony of an absolute desert to feast our eyes upon, with nothing but bacon and beans and rice and bread *and sand* – or rather *sand and bacon*, etc., to eat, sleeping on shore on a sand drift, eyes, nose, mouth, ears, clothing and bed filled with sand..."

Eventually, Ives met Johnson's party on their return downriver. The two adversaries compared notes and then Ives went on. Two months into the trip and 34 miles further upriver than Johnson had attained, the *Explorer* suffered a mishap from a submerged rock. In a skiff, Ives explored a series of rapids before him, and concluded that the mouth of Black Canyon (about 21 miles below Hoover Dam) was the limit for practical steamer navigation. From there, a road could be built through the rocks to Mormon country.

The Mormons feared that the Johnson and Ives trips were forerunners of a full-scale government attack. They roused the Indians to frustrate Ives and his men on their overland trek toward the Grand Canyon. They sent a spy who pretended to be a lost emigrant. Ives gave him food but no information.

Refitted by mule train, the Ives expedition entered the Grand Canyon at Diamond Creek in early April, 1858. From the mouth of the creek, the men would have their first and only view of the Colorado at river level. In the months ahead, the party struggled with late winter storms and, later, intolerable heat. Sometimes the trails became so narrow that the men were forced to dismount from their mules and crawl on their hands and knees. Other times, the trails wound down into dead-ends. Mules and packs had to be somehow turned around. Then back they would all go, retracing their path, trying to figure out where they had made their mistake.

Drawings made by the expedition's artist reveal an overwhelmingly oppressive landscape where awesome, yawning cliffs press in on a tiny river and still tinier human beings. Dr. Newberry later said that the ancient rock "had ceased to excite a pleasurable scientific interest and had even produced a positive thirst for *life* – a longing to reach some region where nature's fire had not all burned out." Ives, the soldier, talked about the "depth and gloom of the gaping chasms..." and about the land's resemblance to the "portals of the infernal regions." Grand Canyon was, Ives decided, "a profitless locality."

The Grand Canyon

No one is absolutely sure how the Grand Canyon came to be. The United States National Park Service tells tourists that the Colorado River may always have been there, where we see it today, but that the land around the river uplifted, cutting out the canyon. And then again, the Service continues, a river may once have been at the top, higher than the present canyon rim, cutting down through all the layers to get from the top to where it is now.

"The carving of the Grand Canyon is the work of rains and rivers... Each river has excavated its own gorge and every creek has excavated its gorge. When a shower comes in this land, the rills carve canyons – but a little at each storm; and though storms are far apart and the heavens above are cloudless for most of the days of the year, still, years are plenty in the ages, and an intermittent rill called to life by a shower can do much work in centuries of centuries." *John Wesley Powell* (The Explorations of the Colorado River and Its Canyons)

The river and the rain have had their share of helpers: wind, ice, snow, animals, tree roots and gravity. Spring thaw traps melting snow within the joints of the Kaibab limestone at the top of the canyon. The water freezes and expands, causing pieces of limestone to loosen and tumble into the canyons. Tree roots grow larger, forcing bits of bedrock to break off. Animals dig burrows, scattering soil and exposing new rock. Over and over again the canyons are recreated.

And if the earth is almost five billion years old, then the last two billion years of its geological and biological history are revealed in the layers of rock that make up the Grand Canyon.

The oldest layer is Vishnu Schist, a greenish-black rock found near Lava Falls in the narrow, V-shaped Granite Gorge. Above this ancient rock is tawny-colored Tapeats sandstone, followed by a lighter green Bright Angel shale. Strata upon strata, sometimes there are more than 15 of them, create bands of pink, purple, russet and green.

Color is everywhere, constant yet changing with the time of the day and the weather. Color is only light, but the walls of the canyon play havoc with light because they appear to undulate to a rhythm all their own. Mirror-slick palisades suddenly turn jagged; walls push out over the chasm, then pull back just as abruptly. Rock stretches itself out, terrace upon terrace, then sucks itself in, into crevices and cave-like sockets.

It's as if an extra-terrestrial being has been at work; a giant stonecutter who, with one hand, carves out an almost incomprehensible expanse of maddening beauty, and who, with his other hand, paints it with an equal sweep of perversity.

In his diary, Major Powell mentions, again and again, the awesome stone arches, alcoves, mounds and pinnacles, under which his wooden boats pass. Before his voyage ended on August 30, he would give names to more natural features along the banks of the Colorado than any person before or since. And all of his names appear on maps today.

On May 27, three days after his voyage began, Powell described a Green River canyon as a "flaring, brilliant red portal." Immediately, he dubbed it *Flaming Gorge*. On a June night, further down the Green, he named the gloomy but strangely beautiful canyon that stretched ahead *Lodore*, after a wild waterfall in the north of England.

By July 17 they had entered the Colorado, passing through the rough waters of Cataract Canyon. The first 61 miles were characterized by nearly vertical walls which seemed to be set with brilliant gems. "We find fountains," Powell said, "bursting from the rock high overhead, and the spray in the sunshine forms the gems which bedeck the walls." Powell thought the shining rock was marble and named this first section of the Grand Canyon *Marble Gorge*. It was later determined that the walls were made of Redwall limestone, but the name remains.

August 13, the expedition camped near the mouth of the Little Colorado River. With the roar of the river ever in their ears, Major Powell and his crew wondered what lay ahead. "Our boats," the Major wrote, "are chafing each other, as they are tossed by the fretful river... We have but a month's rations remaining... We have an unknown distance yet to run; an unknown river yet to explore... With some eagerness, and some anxiety, and some misgiving, we enter the canyon below, and are carried along by the swift water."

That day, Powell couldn't forsee that three of his crew would leave the expedition. But after the Howland brothers and William Dunn climbed up the rocks, he named that place *Separation Canyon* and the waters they wouldn't run, *Separation Rapid*.

The Major was a man who knew what he wanted. A self-taught engineer, geologist and teacher, he funded his first trip through the Grand Canyon from donations and from his own pocket. Congress allocated nothing. But his friend, President Ulysses S. Grant, authorized him to draw rations from army posts. Together, two academic institutions gave him a total of $500; others loaned him scientific instruments. And railroad companies provided free passage for the expedition's personnel and supplies.

Powell and several members of his crew had boating knowledge; no one was skilled in rough water navigation, but if charting the unknown with one arm didn't stop Powell, the river certainly couldn't. A crew member of the Major's second expedition gave this account: "At times we could barely maintain control of the boats so powerful and uninterrupted was the turbulent sweep... At one place as we were being hurled along at a tremendous speed we suddenly perceived immediately ahead of us and in such a position that we could not avoid dashing into it, a fearful commotion of the waters, indicating many large rocks near the surface. The Major stood on the middle deck, his life-preserver in place, and holding by his left hand to the arm of the well-secured chair to prevent being thrown off by the lurching of the boat, peered into the approaching maelstrom. It looked to him like the end for us and he exclaimed calmly, 'By God, boys, we're gone!' With terrific impetus we sped into the seething, boiling turmoil... the Major rapidly giving the orders, 'Left, right, hard on the right, steady, hard on the left... H-A-R-D On The Left, pull away strong.'"

Modern River Runners

Today, from March to October, countless thousands run the Colorado through the Grand Canyon. From 1869 to 1949 only 100 men and two women rode the river. But, with the advent of commercial river-running companies, the numbers increased. In 1966, some 1,000 ran the river; six years later, 17,000. Now, fearful of damage to canyon flora and fauna, the National Park Service limits the yearly traffic.

In oar-maneuvered wooden dories not unlike Major Powell's, or in pontoon rafts powered by an outboard motor, today's runner begins his trip at Lees Ferry, Arizona, just below Glen Canyon Dam. Lees Ferry is an historic site: in 1871, and exiled Mormon murderer, John D. Lee, began making a living by ferrying people and goods across the Colorado at one of the few spots where the river is not hemmed in by high cliffs.

Lees Ferry is Mile 0. At the end of the run, Lake Mead is Mile 280. In between, the runner travels entirely inside the inner gorge of the canyon. Depending on the length and itinerary of his trip, he might stop at the Phantom Ranch, located on the north bank, down the Kaibab and Bright Angel Trails, or at the Hualapai Indian Reservation, inside the canyon, at Diamond Creek.

Always wearing a life preserver, the runner rides the river from three to six hours a day and soon learns to shift his weight to trim the boat. Following the example of the boatsman, he begins to learn how to read the river, how to look for "holes" or gaps between underwater rocks, how to find the smooth tongue of water on which the boat slips into the rapids.

The first, Badger Creek Rapids, is at Mile 8; Soap Creek Rapids is at Mile 11. The rapids are hardly more than 200 yards long, but the runner hears them in the distance.

As the boat climbs up, then rides over and through the waves, the runner is slapped and drenched. The water is 52 degrees Fahrenheit. The runner hasn't time to notice it; he has to start bailing with the little bucket that's been placed by his feet. Besides, the air is dry and hot: June through August, the heat in the canyon, which often reaches 100 to 115 degrees Fahrenheit, soon dries him out.

Day hikes in the side canyons offer more surprise in the form of fern-bordered pools, waterfalls and wildflowers. The animals are hidden in the canyon, but they're there: bighorn sheep, wild mules (left behind by the Spaniards, trappers and prospectors), blue heron, hawks and rattlesnakes. Along the banks of the river, the tamarisk waves its purple sprays, the brittlebush offers yellow blooms, and the ocotilla a display of crimson flowers.

Back on the river, the runner faces Crystal (Mile 98) and Lava Falls (Mile 179), which are the world's fastest navigable rapids. Because of the volcanic flow that once blocked this part of the canyon, the water rages in and out of the holes created by the black rock. Lava Falls has a drop of 37 feet, and both the runner and the boatsman spend about an hour studying the rapid from the river bank. If the boatsman decides that the waters are too dangerous, he takes the boat through alone, while the others follow along the bank.

On each run the boatsman rechecks the rapids. A lower water level means that more rocks are exposed, and that the rapids are more dangerous. The water level varies because 12 miles above Lees Ferry, at Glen Canyon Dam, the Water and Power Resources Service controls the release of water into the river below. The amount varies with demands for electricity or with the levels the service must maintain in the adjacent Lake Powell reservoir. Sometimes the river has the last word. April through June of 1977, a serious drought reduced the flow below the dam to a trickle; in June and July of 1983 an unusually heavy and late spring runoff sent water crashing over the spillways and through the flood gates.

During these years the Colorado returned to its ancient, quixotic self. But most of the time Cataract Canyon in Utah and Grand Canyon in Arizona represent two of the few sections of the Colorado which Major Powell would recognize. The rest of his wild, untamed river has evolved into a vast plumbing system, replete with ditches, dams, flumes, laterals, reservoirs, canals and diversion systems.

The Southwest is desert country. And the one shining star is the Colorado River which, with its several tributaries, brings water and hydroelectric power to the inhabitants of seven states and of northern Mexico.

The Colorado system produces an annual flow that averages between 13-15 million acre feet. (An acre foot is the volume of water required to cover an acre of land to a depth of one foot – about 325,000 gallons.) This sounds like a lot. But take a look at other rivers: the Colorado's flow equals that of the Delaware River, but the former drains a much larger area. The Columbia River in Washington has a watershed similar in size to the Colorado basin, but the Columbia has an estimated flow of 180 million acre feet. The conclusion is obvious, and Major Powell saw it over a hundred years ago: water in the West is not limitless!

As the second director of the United States Geological Survey, Powell tried to impose on the West specific policies regarding settlement and water use, knowing that whoever controlled the land must first control the water, and that whoever controlled the water would determine how the land was to be developed. Powell wanted settlement delayed until the land could be sensibly divided into watersheds, depending on whether it was cropland, pasture, timber country, etc. He also wanted a publicly accountable authority to manage the use of Colorado water.

The West would have none of it. The Colorado was *theirs* – to have and to hold and to use as they saw fit!

Powell kept trying. "Gentlemen," he began, at the National Irrigation Congress of 1893, "... you are piling up a heritage of conflict and litigation of water rights, for there is not sufficient water to supply the land."

The Major was lucky. He was only booed. In 1904, a federal representative pushing for a coordinated development of the lower Colorado was tarred and feathered by California farmers in the newly-created Imperial Valley. We'll manage on our own, thank you very much, said the farmers. And they went ahead and built community and company-owned dikes and levees.

But the River had a mind of its own. In the 1880s and 90s there were alternate periods of drought and flash flood. In the spring of 1905, both the Colorado and Gila rivers rampaged several times, rushing over the levees and flooding the Imperial Valley. Year after year, there was either too much water or so little that armed patrols had to protect what was left in the canals from theft. The farmer was helpless. He needed a stable water supply – a system which strained out the Colorado's silt, stored extra water for dry years and held back spring floods.

Water congresses were formed. Their members emphatically declared that the progress and prosperity of the Southwest depended on the development of the Colorado River's resources. They lobbied in Washington for the construction of dams.

Now the battle over water took a new turn: how much water should each basin state have? In 1922, in the Colorado River Compact, the states within the Colorado River basin agreed to divide the water between the upper states (Colorado, Utah and Wyoming) and the lower ones (California, Nevada, Arizona and New Mexico). A determined amount of acre-feet would go to each state, and the flow from the upper to the lower basin would be measured at Lees Ferry.

Arizona refused to ratify the compact. The unwritten water law of the West says: "Use it or lose it." That means that if the present owner of the water can't use his rightful share, the water passes on to the next one who can. California's burgeoning farm valleys and ever-more-populated cities meant that it would get the water which Arizona couldn't use.

Arizona claimed that circumstances favored California. There was Hoover, the big flood control dam scheduled for Black Canyon, the All-American Canal feeding the Imperial and Coachella valleys, and Parker Dam, designed to generate electricity and carry Colorado water via aqueducts to and for Los Angeles. In 1934, Governor Moor called out the Arizona National Guard to halt the building of Parker Dam. Construction was stalled for 11 months.

The conflict between politics and water rights was finally resolved. The Central Arizona Project was born, and in late 1985, Arizona will begin to utilize fully its legal share of Colorado water. A network of pumps, dams and canals will send water over mountains and desert to Phoenix and eventually on to Tucson, irrigating a million acres of arid land.

This reality, in turn, worries the Arizona Indian Nation. They're afraid that once the "green light" is on, they won't receive their share of water. For the 1922 compact never made allowances for Indian water rights.

In the beginning the farmer battled nature. Ironically, once that battle was won, new conflicts arose. States fought states and Indian Nations. Environmentalists do battle with water and electrical power brokers. (Groups like the Sierra Club lost when Glen Canyon was flooded for the 1964 dam, but they stopped the construction of two dams proposed for sites inside the Grand Canyon.) In 1972 two sovereign nations bickered over the "saltiness" of Colorado water: Mexico complained that the 1.5 million acre-feet of water which flows across its border was so salty that it was ruining Mexican crops. The United States built a desalination plant at Yuma, at great cost to the American taxpayer.

Below Mexico's Morelos Dam the Colorado becomes a muddy creek, then a muddy puddle. In wet years, the river returns to the ancient channel it carved to the gulf. In dry years, it dies in the salt flats.

But, regardless of flood years and drought years, the dammed and spigotted Colorado endures. And what it has created is much more impressive than anything man has done anywhere.

"In the Grand Canyon there are thousands of gorges like that below Niagara Falls, and there are a thousand Yosemites. Yet all these canyons unite to form one grand canyon, the most sublime spectacle on the earth. Pluck up Mt. Washington by the roots to the level of the sea and drop it head first into the Grand Canyon, and the dam will not force its waters over the walls. Pluck up the Blue Ridge and hurl it into the Grand Canyon, and it will not fill it." *John Wesley Powell* (Exploration of the Colorado River of the West and Its Tributaries).

Previous and these pages: near its mountain source in the upper reaches of the Kawuneeche Valley, in Rocky Mountain National Park, the mighty Colorado is little more than a stream. At the foot of the valley the young river spills first into Shadow Mountain Lake (overleaf right) and then Lake Granby (overleaf left), artificial lakes in the Arapaho National Recreation Area.

Above: early morning mist drifts across Grand Lake, more than 8,000 feet up in the Colorado Rockies. Facing page: motor boats moored to a small jetty on the mirror-smooth waters of Lake Granby. Near Parshall, the Colorado passes through Byers Canyon (overleaf left), the first of many canyons it will encounter on its run to the sea. Overleaf right: an Amtrack train follows the Colorado through the mountains near Radium.

Top left: a small tributary of the Colorado which joins the main river below Kremmling. Left: rich cattle pasture near Radium. Above and facing page: the broadening river flows between hills near Burns. Top right: the Colorado near Glenwood Canyon. Overleaf: in Glenwood Canyon there are many small falls both natural (left) and artificial, (right) the Shoestone Dam.

Previous pages: (left) rapids in Glenwood Canyon, about 3 miles below the Shoestone Falls, and (right) Deadhorse Creek tumbles into Glenwood Canyon to meet the Colorado. Below: the First National Bank in Grand Junction. Remaining pictures: Glenwood Springs: (right) Hot Springs Pool, (bottom left) Hot Springs Lodge and the Colorado, (bottom right) Grand Avenue and (facing page) Hot Springs Lodge and the town at night.

Forty miles after flowing into Utah, the Colorado runs alongside Arches National Park, which contains some of the most spectacular rock formations in the world: (left and overleaf left) Delicate Arch; (bottom left) North Window; (below) Balancing Rock; (bottom right) The Windows and La Sal Mountains; (facing page) Skyline Arch and (overleaf right) South Window.

Previous pages: Castle Rock, near Moab. Facing page: Main Street in Moab. Above, top left, top right and overleaf left: the Colorado near Big Bend, northeast of Moab. Right: the river near Moab. Overleaf right: a long ridge of rock runs along Castle Valley towards the distant La Sal Mountains.

44

These pages: spectacular aerial views of Moab and its majestic setting. Fifteen miles downstream from Moab the Colorado flows through Canyonlands National Park which includes (overleaf) the parallel ridges and depressions of the Needles District, formed by the erosion of salt beds beneath the rock.

Above: an aerial view of the river below Spanish Bottom. Facing page: the Colorado near the mining works at the aptly named Potash. Overleaf: inflatable rafts cross the murky waters of Lake Powell, an artificial stretch of water some 180 miles long which was formed when the Glen Canyon Dam was built in 1964.

Facing page: the high rock walls beside the Imperial Rapids. Top right: Lake Powell. Above: the still waters of Dark Canyon, flooded by Lake Powell. Right and top left: a narrow, tranquil side channel of Lake Powell, near Hite Marina. Overleaf: Lake Powell, (left) near Imperial Canyon and (right) near Dark Canyon.

Perhaps one of the best ways to view the wonders of the Colorado is by raft. These pages: various scenes from an overnight stop at Spanish Bottom on one such raft trip. Overleaf: one of the more exhilarating moments of a raft cruise as The Slide is negotiated.

This page: various views around The Loop, which lies above the confluence with the Green River and is one of the more tortuous meanders of the Colorado River. Facing page: the Colorado 3 miles downstream from The Loop.

Just downriver of the confluence of the Green and Colorado Rivers, the waters become wild and dangerous as they plunge into Cataract Canyon (these pages). Overleaf: (left) Goose Neck and Dead Horse Point and (right) the Colorado below Little Bridge Canyon.

Left: the comparatively gentle rapids of The Slide, above The Confluence. Remaining pictures and overleaf: the more turbulent waters of Cataract Canyon which can present a major hazard to rafters. Overleaf: the rapids below Spanish Bottom.

Bottom left: the long-abandoned Indian ruins of Indian Creek, which are thought to date from about AD 1200. Bottom right: the Colorado near Indian Creek. Remaining pictures: a temporary campsite in Lathrop Canyon. Overleaf: two aerial views of the Colorado; (left) northwards from above Sheep Bottom and (right) at Dead Horse Point.

Top left: Dead Horse Point as seen from the river. Left: a prominent rock formation below Little Bridge Canyon. Top right: the river near Wild Horse Canyon. Above: Lathrop Canyon. Facing page: the Claret Cup Cactus blooms on the banks of the Colorado. Overleaf: (left) a view west across Goose Neck and (right) a nearby scene.

These pages: the gentler side of the Colorado: (top left) the river near Jackson Hole; (left and above) smooth waters at Shafer Basin; (top right) Goose Neck Bend and (facing page) a small inflatable at Williams Bottom.

This page: the awesome, sheer walls of Cataract Canyon rise precipitously from the river. In just one mile of this canyon the river drops a staggering 30 feet, creating some of the most ferocious rapids in the world. Facing page: the confluence of the Green and Colorado Rivers.

Top left: the flooded river near Rock Canyon. Top right and facing page: the graceful arch of the bridge carrying State Highway 95 across the Colorado at Hite Marina. Above: Lake Powell near Hite Marina. Right: the canyon of the Dirty Devil River, inundated by Lake Powell. Overleaf: the impressive rock formations of Monument Valley.

Previous pages and facing page: Lake Powell near Wahweap Marina. Top left and top right: Glen Canyon Dam, which holds back the nine trillion gallons of water in Lake Powell. Above: the swimming pool of Wahweap Lodge Motel. Right: Lake Powell near Wahweap Marina.

Facing page and above: the rugged scenery five miles southwest of Page,
Arizona. Right: the Echo Cliffs and United States Highway 89, 30 miles
south of Page. Top: at Bitter Springs the flat, level plain almost hides
the yawning chasm of the Colorado Canyon from view.

About ten million years ago the entire region which now makes up Canyon Country, spreading over the three states of Colorado, Utah and Arizona, began to rise. In a relatively short geologic period of time the great plateau was raised more than a mile above its original position. As the ground rose the rivers and streams of the region cut down through the rock as they struggled to maintain the original levels. The Colorado is one of these rivers and, together with its tributaries, has gouged out the mighty Grand Canyon (these pages and overleaf).

Downstream of Bitter Springs the Colorado plunges down into the depths of the Grand Canyon, its most famous wonder: (facing page) an aerial view near Point Sublime; (top left and top right) views around the Watchtower at Desert View; (left and overleaf left) Crystal Rapids; (above) the formation known as Cheops Pyramid and (overleaf right) the scene west of Crystal Rapids.

The Grand Canyon: (previous pages left) Crystal Rapids; (previous pages right) Bright Angel Canyon; (facing page) Vishnu Temple; (left) Isis Temple; (below) Brahma Temple; (bottom left) Howlands Butte; (bottom right) "Snoopy's Rock" and (overleaf) views near Vishnu Temple.

These pages: two spectacular views of the Grand Canyon from Yaki Point; (above) one hour after dawn and (facing page) just before sunset. Overleaf: the massive edifice of the 726-foot-high Hoover Dam straddles the Nevada-Arizona state line near Boulder City.

Previous pages: (left) Hoover Dam and (right) the Black Canyon just below the dam. Right, below, bottom left and facing page: the moorings of Lake Mead Marina, boating and fishing being popular pastimes on this 115-mile-long lake. Bottom right and overleaf: the mighty Hoover Dam which traps the waters of Lake Mead and provides hydro-electric power.

Top left: seen from Arizona, a casino stands on the Nevada bank of the Colorado near Laughlin. Top right: the Hoover Dam. Left and above: sailing craft and windsurfers near Hemenway Harbor on Lake Mead. Facing page: the shores of Lake Mead near Las Vegas Wash.

These pages: Lake Havasu, which was formed in 1938 with the construction of Parker Dam; (top left) English Village, (left) the stern-wheeler *River Queen* moored at the Waterfront, (above) Lake Havasu Golf Course, (top right) the Waterfront and (facing page) sunset over the lake.

Lake Havasu City: (above and top left) the English Village, a replica of rural English shops and pubs; (top right) the Queens Bay Hotel and (above and facing page) the stern-wheeler *River Queen* and London Bridge.

Left, bottom left, bottom right and facing page: the 150-year-old London Bridge which was rebuilt stone-by-stone at Lake Havasu in 1971 and brings a genuine touch of England to Arizona. Below: a quiet backwater on Lake Havasu. Overleaf: the Colorado just north of Yuma.

INDEX